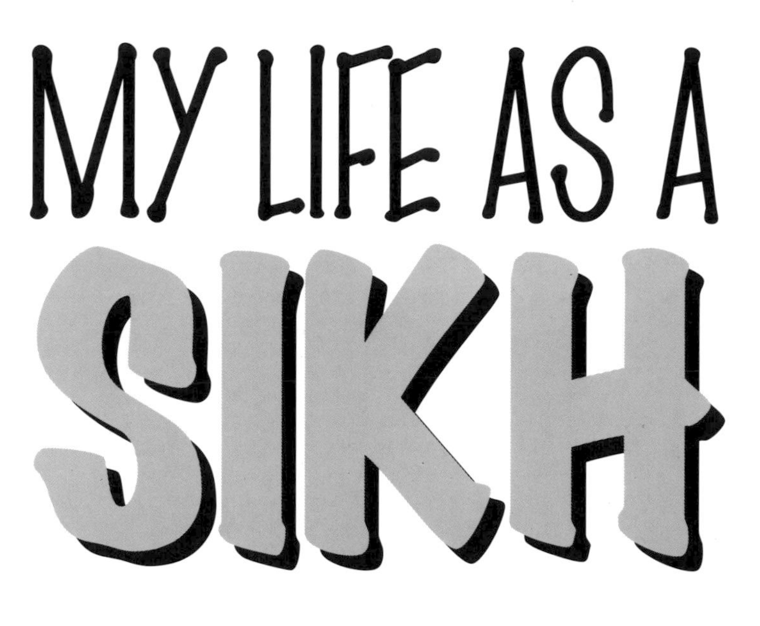

• Trevo[illegible]
• Sue M[illegible]
• Paul Morga[illegible]

DREF WEN

The Mool Mantra

There is one God,
Eternal Truth is his Name:
Maker of all things,
Fearing nothing and hating nothing.
He is timeless and without form;
Not begotten, being of his own Being;
By the grace of the Guru, made known to men.

Special Photography Pat and Charles Aithie (ffotograff)

Design Michael Leaman Design Partnership

The books in this series are also available in Welsh-language editions.

Photographs Trevor Guy (ESIS) pages 8 top, 26 foot, 27 right; Nick Tapsell (ffotograff) front cover centre right, pages 10/11 foot. All other photographs are by Pat and Charles Aithie (ffotograff). Some of these (often indicated by corner mountings) are reproduced from photographs kindly provided by the families concerned. *Map* Pat and Charles Aithie (ffotograff) page 6. We have made every effort to contact owners of copyright material and apologise if in any instance we have been unsuccessful.

First published 1999 by Gwasg y Dref Wen, 28 Church Road, Whitchurch, Cardiff CF4 2EA. Telephone 01222 617860.

Printed in Hong Kong.

Contents

My community

Sunny: *My favourite things are drawing and playing on the computer.*

SUNNY My name is Gurdeep **Singh** Lyall, but my nickname is Sunny. I've been called Sunny since I was born. I live in Cardiff and go to school at Marlborough Road Juniors. I've got lots of friends: Daniel, Tom, Sabah who's a Muslim, and Naseem, Claire, Sarah and James. I like art and technology because I enjoy making things. I like playing football and playing with the computer. I have just started scouts. I go to the same **gurdwara** as Neena. I'm learning to speak Punjabi so I can read the holy book and also because that's what most people speak at our gurdwara. For me going to the gurdwara is like belonging to a family. It's also like a church because you go there to pray and I meet my Sikh friends who go to different schools.

Sunny: *I've been learning to play the tabla for 6 months. My dad helps me sometimes.*

Neena: *I enjoy meeting friends at the gurdwara.*

THINK ABOUT:

Why do you think Sunny says belonging to the Sikh community is like belonging to a family?

What does Neena like about the gurdwara?

Apart from school, where are the places you like going to meet other people?

Neena: I love music. I like to play and I sing. I write down the words of songs and learn them.

FACT FILE

Singh All Sikh males can use this name after their first names. Singh means "lion".

Gurdwara A Sikh temple where people go to worship. The word means "house of the guru".

Kaur All Sikh females can use Kaur after their first name. It means "princess". In this way all Sikh people are joined together by their names, like the people in a family.

NEENA I'm Neena **Kaur** Baicher. I live in Magor in South Wales and go to school in Caerleon. It's good. I like going to school. I like drama and I'm better at language than science. I have friends at school but the gurdwara is the main place for me. I get on so well with everyone over there. Everyone knows you and you grow up with your childhood friends at the gurdwara. Everyone goes there week after week. When new families move into the area and come to the gurdwara, it's a chance to meet them and make more friends.

Sunny: This is Mum with my sister Joyti.

THINGS TO DO

What are the things you enjoy doing with your family? Write about them or draw them.

Is there a place you go where you feel especially happy or "at home"? Draw and write about the place you most like to be.

Sharing a name is one way in which Sikhs feel part of their community. This also helps to give them their identity. Think of a community you belong to (perhaps your family, school or a group) and write about what helps you to feel you belong. What do you do or wear to show you are a member of this community?

How my religion began

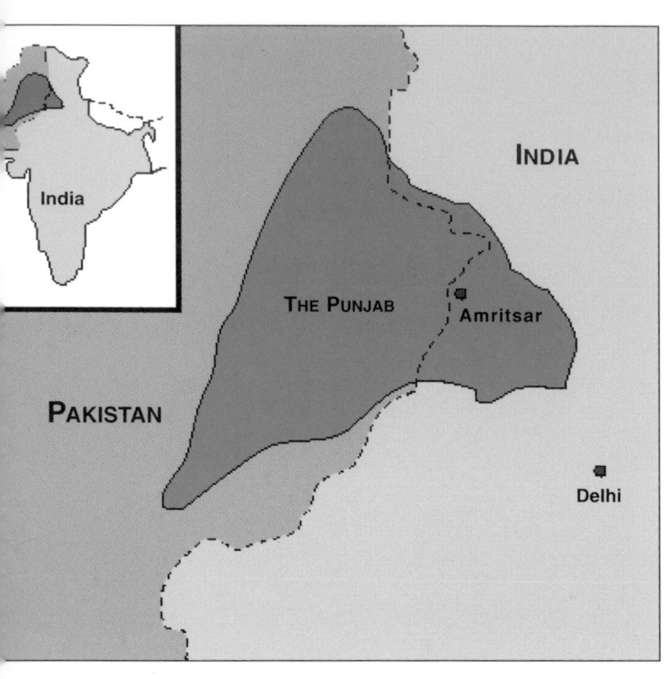

This is the part of India where Guru Nanak was born. It is called the Punjab.

NEENA Each Sunday morning, Sunny and I go to the Punjabi class at the gurdwara. The children are split into four classes and we are both in class three. This is what our teacher told us about how our religion began:

Guru Nanak was our first **guru**. He was born in India nearly 500 years ago. Nanak was a thoughtful man. He tried to understand what God was like and to do what God wanted. We call ourselves Sikhs because that means "followers" of the guru. We try to learn from our gurus and to follow their teaching about God.

Guru Nanak explained that there is only one God and that he is the creator of all life. He told people that because God made everyone, we must love everyone equally. Men and women, black people and white, people from all countries and all religions are equal in God's eyes.

Our holy book, the **Guru Granth Sahib**, is full of hymns and poems written by Guru Nanak and the other gurus. It also has writings by **Hindu** and **Muslim saints**. This is because the Guru went everywhere and met all sorts of people in search of the truth about God. Whenever Nanak found someone who could help him, he was glad to listen. He said, "Everywhere you go, everywhere you look, God is there."

THINK ABOUT:

What does "guru" mean?

How do Sikhs show that the Guru Granth Sahib is important to them? You will find more information on pages 10-11, 20-21 and 22.

Why does the Sikh holy book contain writings by people who are not Sikhs?

Children learn Punjabi at the gurdwara so they can read the Guru Granth Sahib. Punjabi is the language spoken in the Punjab.

Pictures of the gurus are found in the gurdwara and in many Sikh homes. Guru Nanak is in the middle at the top.

Fact file

Guru A name for a religious teacher in India.

Guru Granth Sahib The word Granth means "a big book". The word Sahib is used to show respect. It is like the English word "Sir".

Hindu A person whose religion is Hinduism. Hindus worship God in the form of many different gods and goddesses. Hinduism is the main religion of India and Guru Nanak was brought up as a Hindu.

Muslim A person whose religion is Islam. Islam is found in many countries, including India. Muslims believe there is only one God, whom they call Allah.

Saint A person who has led a very holy life, living as he or she thinks God wants.

When Guru Nanak died, other gurus carried on his teaching and became our leaders. When Guru Gobind Singh, our last guru, died, he did not choose another leader for us. Instead he told us the holy book would be our teacher and guru. That is why we call our holy book the Guru Granth Sahib.

Neena and Sunny in the Punjabi class.

Things to do

Draw a picture of or describe the person who has taught you most and given you the best advice or help. If you draw a picture, write a sentence about this person.

Is there a book which has taught you something important or helped your understanding? Write a review of your book and say why it is important to you.

Do you have an idea of what sort of person Guru Nanak was after reading this? Imagine you have met him and write a letter to a friend describing him and what he did and believed.

Starting out in life

Something sweet is traditionally eaten to celebrate the birth of a Sikh baby. If the family don't have ladoos or barfi they may put out a bowl of sugar. Sharing the sweetness is like wishing a blessing on the baby.

SUNNY When my cousin Harjot was born there was a big party and everyone was given some special sweets called ladoos. There are other sweets like barfi you might be given, but the ladoos are usual.

SUNNY'S MUM In the Sikh community we don't name our babies until they are 40 days old. Most people just call them "baby" until then. In this country people in the hospital usually ask you the baby's name straight after the baby is born. So we choose a name for the baby until it gets its proper name at the gurdwara. The name "Sunny" reminds me of light. He was born in the morning and Sunny just came into my mind.

Soon after the baby has been born the father or someone else from the family will go to the gurdwara. The **Granthi** will read the holy book and give the family a letter of the alphabet that will start the baby's name. You can choose the name then if you like or you can take up to 40 days. If the father has a sister, she will usually be asked to choose the baby's name. It is a way of making her feel special. You usually find that this aunty is very close to the children.

Neena: *Here I am with my brother Vikram when he was a baby. He was born on Guru Nanak's birthday so that is considered very important and special.*

Neena: *When the Granthi gives the first letter for the baby's name from the Holy Book, it is as though God has helped to choose it.*

THINK ABOUT:

What part does the holy book have in welcoming Sikh babies into their community?

Why is the present of a Rumala so special?

Why is it important to share something sweet when a Sikh baby is born?

The Guru Granth Sahib is wrapped in cloths called Rumalas.

Fact file

Granthi The name for the person who takes care of the Guru Granth Sahib or holy book, and leads the worship in the gurdwara by reading from it. The Granthi also takes the holy book out of the gurdwara for events like weddings.

Turban A long piece of cloth worn by Sikh men to cover their hair.

Rumala A specially made piece of cloth which is wrapped around the Guru Granth Sahib.

On the 13th day after the baby has been born, the Granthi comes to your home and brings the holy book with him. He reads from the book to bless the baby and the mother. The family makes a lovely meal to welcome the Granthi and give him a gift of material for a new suit and a new **turban** length.

At 40 days the child is taken to the gurdwara for blessing. That's when it's given its name. The baby is given a gift from the congregation of a **Rumala** that has been used to wrap the holy book. That makes it very special. So the mother takes it home and keeps it among the baby's clothes and in that way the baby is blessed.

Sunny: *Rumalas are decorated with silvery and golden thread.*

Things to do

What gift would you give to your family and friends to show you were glad to have a new baby in the family? Draw it or write about it and say why you have chosen it.

Design a Rumala to wrap around the holy book. Use patterns connected with the Sikhs in your design. You will find pictures in this book helpful to start your ideas.

Do you know how your name was chosen? Does your name have a meaning? Do you like your name? What name would you have chosen for yourself? Write about your name and try to answer these questions in your work. You may need to do some research at home first.

Following the path

Each day the Guru Granth Sahib is taken out of the room where it is kept and placed on a high seat under a canopy.

NEENA I would say the main thing for us to follow is the Guru Granth Sahib because that has all the teachings in it. It is made up of hymns. It doesn't bother me too much if I don't know exactly what they mean. I think to myself that they mean something good anyway. When I'm listening to them, if I don't understand, I think about the week gone by and reflect on everything that's happened.

We do not worship the Guru Granth Sahib but we do hold it in high honour. The book is our last guru, so we look after it as we would look after any of the human gurus. When it is not being used it rests in a special room of its own.

Our holy book teaches us about God and how we should behave towards God and other human beings. We are taught that all people are equal before God and that we must respect them all.

When the day's services are finished the book is carefully wrapped and put to bed.

THINK ABOUT:

How do Sikhs show that they treat their holy book with as much respect as they would a human being?

Neena often thinks about the week gone by when she listens to the Guru Granth Sahib being read. Why might it be a good idea to reflect on the past week?

Why do you think Sikhs just use the one copy of the Guru Granth Sahib in the Golden Temple from which to copy all other Guru Granth Sahibs?

*The Granthi waves a **chauri** over the book as a mark of respect.*

Cremate To burn. It is one of the ways people dispose of dead bodies.

Chauri A fly whisk. In the old days in India, the chauri was waved like a fan to cool people down and whisk away flies. Only rich and important people could afford to pay someone to do this. So it reminds Sikhs how important the holy book is.

We use the Guru Granth Sahib in all our services. It is also used when we celebrate special days, at weddings, and when we give babies their names, or welcome people into a new home. On many occasions we read the book from start to finish. It takes a team of readers 48 hours to do this without stopping.

We care for the holy book as we would care for people. When it is too old or damaged to use, it goes to a special gurdwara to be **cremated**.

This is the most important gurdwara. It is the Golden Temple at Amritsar. A very old, hand-written copy of the Guru Granth Sahib is kept here. All modern copies are made from this one.

THINGS TO DO

Draw a Guru Granth Sahib on its seat under a canopy.

The Guru Granth Sahib teaches Sikhs about respect for all human beings. Design a poster showing how people can show respect for each other.

Imagine you are a Granthi. Write about one day in your life, including what you have to do with the Guru Granth Sahib.

What we believe

NEENA We have a special saying, "I kum kal, sat nam." This means, "There is only one God, he is the creator and truth is his name." I've come to believe this. I think there *is* only one God and he can't belong to anybody. He created everyone and they're all equal no matter whether they're one religion or another religion. I don't have a clear idea of what God is like. I believe God is like a power or a spirit. That's what I personally believe. I don't know if that's what all Sikhs think.

I have a real feeling that God can do things in my life. I often have the feeling there really is someone there watching over me. If I have a test, I'll pray just before it as if to say, "I'm doing something important now, I need help." And when I'm in bed at night and I sometimes get scared, I pray because I believe that saying this prayer will help me.

Preparing food, serving it and clearing away afterwards are signs of service.

THINK ABOUT:

What sort of things does Neena think God can do in her life?

Why would Sikhs think it is important to meditate?

Neena prays for help sometimes. On what occasions do you ask for help and who do you ask?

Sunny: *We believe it is important to serve others; this is called Sewa. At the gurdwara you might see people dusting and tidying up the shoes which people take off as they enter the building.*

SUNNY

My mum told me a well-known Sikh story. It shows what we believe about work and about treating people well:

> *Once Guru Nanak went to visit a place. While he was there he stayed with a poor holy man. He had no money but the Guru chose to stay with him because he was a man of God. In the same town lived a very rich landowner. He was angry that Nanak choose to stay with such a poor, unimportant person.*
>
> *Guru Nanak said, "Each of you bring me an offering and then I will decide who to stay with." They both brought a coin, and the Guru held one in each hand. Then he squeezed them. From the poor man's offering came sweet, fresh milk. From the rich man's offering came blood. The rich man was shocked and asked why this had happened. Nanak explained that his offering had been earned from the sufferings of the poor, but the poor man's offering had come from his own honest efforts.*

FACT FILE

Meditate To think deeply and carefully about something. Many religious people spend time thinking about God in this way.

Neena: *The older people get peace of mind at the gurdwara. Sometimes they ask us to be quiet if we are making a noise. They want to rest and think. All Sikhs are supposed to* ***meditate****.*

THINGS TO DO

Write a list of five Sikh beliefs and present them neatly with coloured decoration or by using the computer.

Write about the kind of life Sikhs should lead if they follow their beliefs.

The story about the rich man and the poor man is a parable, a story used to explain an important idea. Write and illustrate a parable of your own to explain the idea of serving other people.

Neena: *A newly-married couple have to learn to get on with each other. Parents need to be there to guide their children. I really get upset when I hear about a divorce.*

Right and wrong

SUNNY The main thing that helps me decide what is right and wrong is what my mum and dad say. You should always listen to what your parents say. You should also do what God tells you. I know some things are wrong, like smoking, because I've seen it's bad for your health and can kill you. I believe you should not hurt anyone, by the things you do or the things you say.

NEENA Most of the time I make up my own mind about what is right and what is wrong. I think to myself, "What would Dad do in this position?" He lists all the bad points and all the good points about something so he can work out what is the right thing to do. If it's really tough to decide what is the right thing to do, I might do a bit of praying and ask, "What shall I do now?"

Neena: *Life is a bit like playing tennis. If you don't keep to the rules, you can't really enjoy it.*

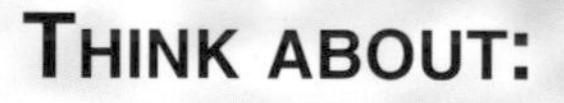

THINK ABOUT:

What do you think is the worst thing a person can do?

What do you see happening in the world which upsets you because you think it is wrong?

Are there any of Sunny's or Neena's beliefs about right and wrong which you agree or disagree with? Why?

Sunny: *We shouldn't dump things in the sea and should be careful that things like oil tanker disasters don't happen again.*

Sunny: *We must look after our world.*

I think people should try not to be angry and to be more tolerant of each other. The Guru Granth Sahib tells us that. The world can't be perfect but if people would try to be more tolerant it would be a lot better. If I've said something which I shouldn't have to someone, I just go up to them and say sorry. Some people feel as if they are swallowing their pride when they do that, but I don't feel like that.

I think God is hurt when people do wrong. I've always had this idea that God feels sad when we do things that are wrong.

Things to do

Make a list of five things that you think are really wrong.

Make a list of things people could do to make the world a better place. Choose one or two of your ideas and explain them more fully. Draw pictures to go with what you write.

Sunny talks about not hurting other people. Neena describes feeling sorry about telling people off when she shouldn't have. They are both talking about tolerance. Look up the word "tolerance" in your dictionary. Write a short story, real or imagined, about a time when you showed tolerance, even though it was difficult to do so.

Sunny: *You've got to keep your hair clean because a Sikh has to be clean and pure on the outside as well as on the inside.*

Daily life

NEENA The first thing that lets people know I'm a Sikh is my name, Neena Kaur Baicher. Kaur means princess. When people at school ask me why I have Kaur in my name I say, "Well it's part of my Sikh identity and all Sikh girls have that name." They usually say, "Oh that's good, isn't it?", because my name also tells people what my religion is.

Another thing is your hair. One of my friends has hair that comes right down her back. People ask her why she wears it like that and she says, "I don't cut my hair because of my religion." She feels proud of it. I think that's really good. It shows other young people what you think about yourself.

My mum and dad don't mind what I wear really. They say we are living in modern Britain so I should dress like other girls the same age as me. I wouldn't wear anything really short but that's mainly my personality.

When you go to someone's house you say, "Sat siri akal," which means "Truth is supreme." My dad says it's to show that there is one true God. You use it to say hello and goodbye.

THINK ABOUT:

What things help Sunny and Neena feel sure of their identity as Sikhs?

Why do Sikh men wear a patkah or a turban?

Are all Sikhs vegetarian? What sorts of things might they take into account when deciding what to eat?

Neena: *When I go to the gurdwara I wear a Punjabi suit. If I had taken* ***Amrit*** *I would wear the Five Ks every day.*

Sunny: Sikhs should be vegetarian. The strict rule is that you shouldn't eat meat unless there is no other way to survive.

Fact File

Dahl Cooked lentils with spices added.

Amrit Taking Amrit is the ceremony Sikhs go through to promise that they will keep their religion strictly and seriously. Having taken Amrit, a Sikh will then wear five special things, called the Five Ks. You can read about these on pages 18 and 19.

SUNNY I wear a patkah, which is a head covering, to keep my hair clean and neat because it has to be kept long. Sometimes people ask if I've got long hair. I don't show them because if the head cover comes off I wouldn't be able to put it back on. When I'm older I may wear a turban.

We eat mostly vegetarian food, potato curry, **dahl** and rice. I'm the only person who eats meat in our house. My sister eats fish but my mum and dad don't. We never eat beef but I like lamb and chicken and pork. Sikhs never eat beef, but not because of mad cow disease. It's for religious reasons. Strict Sikhs will not eat any meat at all.

***Neena:** This is my kara, my religious bracelet. I wear it on my right wrist. All Sikhs are supposed to wear one. I wear mine to protect me from fear.*

Things to do

Design a meal that a strict Sikh could share with you. You could write or draw your ideas.

What makes you feel proud of yourself? Is it something you wear or something you have done? Perhaps belonging to a community like your family or class made you feel proud at some time. Write about whatever has made you feel like this.

Neena says that wearing her kara protects her from fear. Is there anything you wear or do which helps you not to feel afraid? Explain what it is and why it works for you.

Growing up as a Sikh

Kesh (long hair): *Many Sikhs do not cut their hair because their bodies are created by God. They feel that to cut off part of that body is to be disrespectful to God.*

NEENA When Sikhs feel ready to make a complete commitment to their religion they go through a ceremony called Amrit. I don't know when I'll decide to take Amrit. Perhaps one day something will happen to make me feel I should do it. There's no set time for taking Amrit. Some people take it when they're young and some when they're very old. It really depends on the person.

I think about religion a lot. I know Amrit is very sacred and important but I'm not entirely sure of what will happen to me and what it will mean afterwards. My friend Rapinder has taken it. She is a very calm person and very easy-going. She wasn't worried about it. None of Rapinder's family have taken Amrit but she made up her own mind and just knew it was the right thing for her to do. She now wears the **Five Ks.**

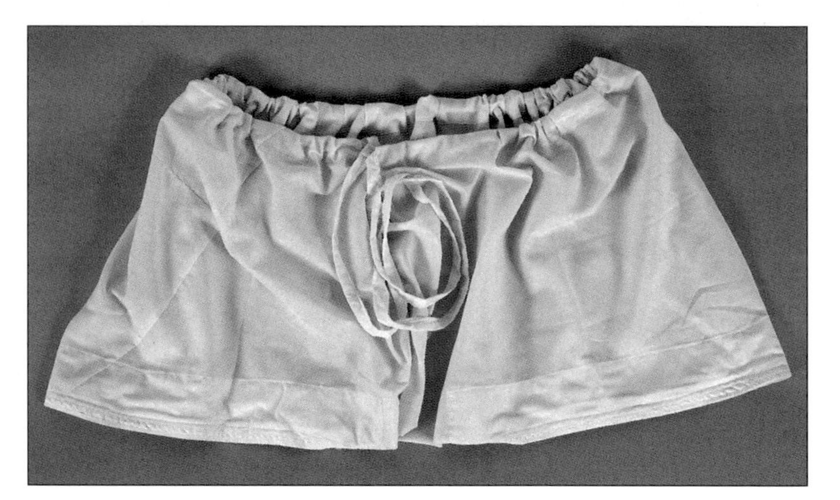

Kachera (shorts): *These are worn by men and women. They are part of the modest dress that Sikhs should wear. Indian clothes at the time of Guru Nanak were wrap-around strips of material. They made it difficult to run or fight at a time when the Sikhs were often fighting for their lives. The kachera gave freedom of movement for the first time.*

THINK ABOUT:

Why did Guru Gobind Singh want the Sikhs to wear the Five Ks and use the surnames Kaur and Singh?

How do you think Sunny will feel when he has his turban tied on for the first time?

Why might Neena be a bit afraid about taking Amrit?

Kangha (wooden comb): *Sikhs believe they should keep a clean, healthy mind in a clean, healthy body. The wooden comb is a sign of this.*

SUNNY When I'm old enough to tie my own turban we'll have a big ceremony in the gurdwara. It's usually when a boy is about 11.

The Guru Granth Sahib is read all the way through, which takes two days. On the third day the boy wears a turban for the first time. His mother's brother ties it on for him. He gets lots of presents and money from the congregation.

FACT FILE

The Five Ks Sikhs who have been confirmed in their faith wear five symbols. The name of each one begins with the letter K, so they have become known as the Five Ks. The symbols were given to the Sikhs by the last guru, Gobind Singh. Each of the Five Ks is pictured on these pages.

Kara *(bangle): The bangle is made of iron or steel. So it is strong and reminds Sikhs to stay strong in their faith. It is also a circle which reminds Sikhs of God who, like a circle, has no beginning and no end.*

THINGS TO DO

Draw each of the Five Ks and name them. Write a sentence about each one.

Is there something you wear which would tell others something about you or your idea of yourself? Draw it and write about it.

What are you looking forward to doing when you are old enough? Is there something you are not allowed to do now but which you think you will enjoy when you get older? Explain what it is and how you think you will feel when you are allowed to do it for the first time.

Kirpan *(sword): This shows that although Sikhs believe in peace, they are willing to stand up and fight for what they know to be right. The sword can be a dangerous weapon, so many Sikhs today carry a very small imitation of the kirpan.*

Worship in the home

Sunny: When my mother prays she remembers how our religion started and mentions all the saints and gurus. We pray for Sikhs in Cardiff and everywhere. Then we ask for blessings and forgiveness and wish peace for the whole world.

SUNNY In the morning and before going to bed, we should pray. We say the Mool Mantra. This is the most important prayer for Sikhs. When you pray you are praising the Lord and asking him for his help. You know that he won't turn his back on you. If you are in trouble you can get some comfort from God.

NEENA We don't have a **Baba Jee** at home, but if we had one, I would probably spend some time in Baba Jee's room before I went to school. I'd pray there because I think I'd get peace of mind from doing that. Some of my friends do have one in their houses. We'd have one if we had the right kind of room we could devote to it.

When there's an important occasion, like someone's birthday or a special celebration, Mum gets up early and comes down to make **prashad**. Then before we go to gurdwara we all come downstairs, Mum says a prayer and we have the prashad.

I pray when I feel I should. If I'm really desperate for help I'll pray all the time. Where my aunt lives in America, the gurdwara is enormous and doesn't feel like a personal place to pray. So lots of people have their own Baba Jee's room with a Guru Granth Sahib in it. It's different for us here in Cardiff. The gurdwara seems so much more personal.

THINK ABOUT:

What can you see on Sunny's mother's worship table? How might each of these things help her to pray?

Why would Neena spend time in Baba Jee's room if her family had one?

Who are some of the people a Sikh might mention in prayer?

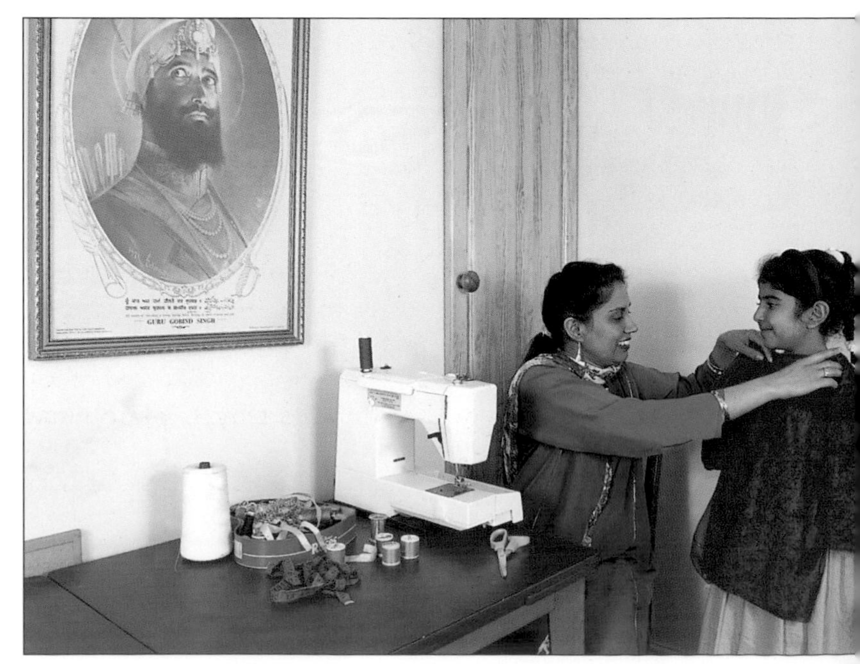

Sunny: There are many pictures of the gurus in all the rooms in our house.

***Sunny:** My mother keeps a special little table in the dining room for her daily worship. She's got several **Gutkas** for the morning prayer. There is also a **diva lamp** and a **joss stick** holder.*

Fact file

Baba Jee Another way of referring to the Guru Granth Sahib. The words mean "respected grandfather". To keep a Guru Granth Sahib at home, Sikhs must have a separate room just for the book.

Prashad A mixture of semolina, sugar and butter which is blessed and shared as a way of sharing in God's gift of food.

Gutka A small book containing some writings from the Guru Granth Sahib.

Diva lamp A small clay lamp containing a candle or filled with oil.

Joss stick A stick of wood coated with perfumes or spices. It burns slowly and gives off a scented smoke.

Things to do

Draw and label what you would find on the worship table.

Neena's mother makes prashad to celebrate special occasions. Is there a special thing you do when you celebrate in your family? Perhaps it will be on birthdays or on Mother's Day. Explain what you do and how it makes you feel.

Write about what gives you comfort if you are in trouble. Would you pray, is there a person you could talk to, or is there something else you would do? You could write your answer as a story or a poem.

Worship in the gurdwara

SUNNY The building where we worship is called a gurdwara. The first thing you must do when you go in is take off your shoes and wash your hands. Everyone must cover their heads as a sign of respect.

When you go into the prayer hall you must bow in front of the book. You put some money down and say a prayer. Unless there are Punjabi classes for the children, we join everybody else to say prayers and sing and listen to the Guru Granth Sahib being read. The men and women sit on separate sides.

Sunny: *The first thing you would notice in the gurdwara would be the stage and canopy with the Guru Granth Sahib.*

Sunny: *As people come in they bow and place an offering in front of the book.*

THINK ABOUT:

What must every person do when they first enter a gurdwara?

What is the most important thing in the gurdwara?

Sikhs share food as part of their worship. Why might they think that sharing food is so important? What do you think and how do you feel when you share food with someone?

Sunny: *Each week someone who has a special reason for saying thank you to God will give food and prepare a meal for everyone to share. This part of the worship is called the langar.*

Sunny: *The prashad is blessed and then shared out. Anyone is welcome to eat in the langar.*

The second part of worship in the gurdwara is the **langar** or sharing of food. A meal is cooked in the kitchen during the first part of the service. A little bit of everything we are going to eat is taken into the prayer hall to be offered to God and blessed. When it has been blessed it is taken back into the kitchen and mixed with the rest of the food so everyone has part of the blessed food in their dinner. Everything we're going to eat or drink, even a glass of water, is blessed.

Everyone is served with some food but no-one eats until the **grace** has been said. I think the best bit is at the end when they have cleared up the food and we are allowed to run around in the hall.

Fact File

Langar The word for the kitchen which is part of every gurdwara. Langar is also the word used for the food which is made in the kitchen. Buying, cooking, serving and sharing food together is a very important part of Sikh worship. It is a way of making everyone feel part of the same family.

Grace A prayer of thanks to God, said before eating.

Things to do

Imagine you are part of a Sikh family. As part of your birthday celebrations, your family will be holding a langar meal for you next week at the gurdwara. Design an invitation card to send to your family and friends.

Write a grace which could be used before a shared meal.

Design a simple leaflet to explain how a visiting class of children should behave in a gurdwara and what they should expect to do and see.

Getting married

Neena: *When the families meet up at the first part of the wedding they usually exchange garlands of flowers. In the Punjab even the car is decorated with flowers.*

NEENA I've been to two weddings. In the first part of the ceremony the two families meet to exchange greetings and gifts. The families wait on opposite sides of a big room. Then the fathers come into the middle and greet each other, then the brothers do likewise and so on.

Next there is the religious part of the ceremony. This is usually led by the Granthi but any Sikh who knows the ceremony could do it. No matter where you go in the world it would be the same. The couple agree to be married by bowing towards the Guru Granth Sahib. The bride's father gives one end of a pink wedding **chuni** to the groom and the other end to the bride. It joins them together as husband and wife. There are four readings from the Guru Granth Sahib and as each of the readings is begun, the bride follows the groom around the Guru Granth Sahib.

Towards the end of the wedding everyone throws confetti or flower petals and the prashad is shared. After the ceremony there is a reception, usually at a hotel or sometimes in the gurdwara if there is a suitable room. No two celebrations are exactly the same.

Just going to the weddings was really good for me. The food was excellent! People gave the couple presents, either money or something for their home: a vase or a blender or something.

THINK ABOUT:

Why do you think Sikhs have the greeting ceremony as the first part of their wedding?

What does the special pink chuni show at the wedding?

Why are weddings such enjoyable occasions?

Sunny: *This is a picture of my aunty and uncle at their wedding. Sikh brides often wear red wedding clothes.*

Neena: *As children we will try to do what our parents want. When it's time to get married, we will listen to their advice, to help us decide on the right person to marry.*

SUNNY I've been to lots of weddings. They sometimes have a party after and then there might be a disco. Once there was a massive balloon full of little balloons. At a certain time they burst it and the grown-ups kept on dancing and stepping on the balloons. It was really good.

FACT FILE

Chuni The long scarf which Sikh women and girls wear to cover their heads.

THINGS TO DO

If you had to take just one photograph of a Sikh wedding what would you take? Draw the scene you think would be the most important or interesting.

Describe a wedding you have seen. Where did the ceremony take place? What kind of celebrations happened afterwards? If you have not been to a wedding, ask your family or friends.

The Sikh couple circle the holy book four times as they hear readings telling them what they should promise each other. Decide on four promises you think a couple should make to each other when they get married. Put them in order of importance, write them out very carefully and decorate your page so that it looks like an important document.

Celebrating festivals

Good Wishes on
Shri Guru Nanak Dev ji's Birthday

Sikh Council

271 Soho Road, Handsworth,
Birmingham B21 9ST Tel: 021-523 5895

***Neena:** At festival times people give each other presents and send each other cards. Everyone also gets a card from the gurdwara.*

NEENA There are two main festivals really: **Divali** and **Baisakhi**. Divali is best in the gurdwara, but I prefer the way we celebrate Baisakhi outside the gurdwara.

At Divali there is a special ceremony when a little tray of lights is waved around. This is called the arti ceremony. On the stage are trays with candles and as people come in they put more candles all over the stage. At Divali you wear white clothes. There's not very much decoration in the gurdwara except that coloured lights are put up.

For Baisakhi last year, we had our big celebration in County Hall. An Indian pop group played and some of the people from the Sikh community entertained everyone as well. Two girls did a classical dance and I did one with a friend that we made up ourselves. Some people played the drums and sang and then there was food. It went on until about twelve o'clock at night.

THINK ABOUT:

How do Sikhs celebrate their festivals?

Why is Baisakhi so important for Sikhs?

Why might sisters and brothers have a day when they give each other a special gift?

***Sunny:** The community organises outings and sports days. I've got some medals from the games that we had for Baisakhi last year.*

In August we have a festival called Rakhery when girls give their brothers a bracelet. Some years we are in India for the festival. It's brilliant there. People make offerings at the gurdwara and eat special sweets.

Fact file

Divali Also celebrated by Hindus as a festival of light. For Sikhs Divali is a time to remember when one of the gurus was in prison. When the emperor decided to release him, he said he would only go if the 52 Hindu princes in the prison were also set free.

Baisakhi A festival held in April which celebrates the time when, in 1699, the last guru, Guru Gobind Singh, formed the Sikh brotherhood. This was to protect all Sikhs from people who were trying to stop them from following their religion.

Sunny: *At Baisakhi we take the flagpole outside the gurdwara down, wash it and change the flag.*

Neena: *A rakhi is a kind of bracelet that girls give their brothers at Rakhery.*

Things to do

Design a rakhi that you could give to a brother, sister or friend. Write one reason why you want to give it to them.

Read or listen to the story of Baisakhi. Write a newspaper account of the events with a headline to sum up the story.

Many festivals celebrate important events that have happened in the past. Think of one important event in history or in your own life Write a short account of the event and how you would like to celebrate that event.

Working for others

SUNNY When the children at Dunblane were killed we collected money at the gurdwara. Another time, a lady came to our school to tell us about an obstacle course we could do to raise money for Age Concern and I got sponsors to do that.

SUNNY'S DAD The gurdwara gives to charities and when there is a disaster. We may decide to give money from the gurdwara funds or to have an appeal to raise money for a good cause.

There are lots of Sikh charities and in a Sikh community you will see people helping every day in all sorts of ways. There is a Sikh **Missionary** Society in Britain and it tries to provide help for people who need it. The Sikh Forum also raises money for good causes.

***Sunny:** Helping with worship and teaching at the gurdwara are some of the ways Sikhs show their belief in working for others.*

THINK ABOUT:

What are some of the ways in which Sikhs work for others?

Why do Sikhs think it is important to help others? What sorts of things do you do for other people? Why do you help others?

What do you think is the most surprising way Sikhs help other people?

Neena: *The langar is a place where everybody is welcome in our community – any race, any colour, any religion.*

Missionary
Someone who, because of religious beliefs, works to help others.

Neena: *Many Sikhs choose work that involves helping others. My mum is a social worker and dad teaches in a college.*

In one gurdwara I know, they cook lunch for the elderly in the community every day. A large gurdwara in Birmingham does a lot for local people. It is open 24 hours a day for anyone who will respect it. If they respect the place and what is going on there, anyone is welcome. The Sikhs there also take food to the homeless.

Helping others and serving others is very important in our religion. The hymns that we sing tell us how we should do this.

THINGS TO DO

If you could start a charity, who would it help? Design a badge for your charity which you could give to people on a collection day. It should show who you are raising money for or why you think people should support you.

Make a list of all the ways you could help other people. Choose one of the things and do it this week. Next week write down what happened and how you felt.

Imagine you are one of the old, lonely or homeless people the Sikh community is helping. What is your life like? How do you feel? Describe what you think and feel when you see some Sikhs from the local gurdwara bringing you food and friendship. You could write this as a poem or story.

Sunny: *After a dead person has been cremated the ashes are sprinkled into water. Here in South Wales they may be taken up into the Brecon Beacons to the source of the water where it is pure.*

What happens when we die?

SUNNY I haven't really thought about what will happen to me when I die. My dad said that what we do in this life will have an effect on what happens to us afterwards. I've never thought about meeting up with people when I die. I've never heard Sikh people talk about that.

SUNNY'S MUM In our teachings we read that there are many lives you lead before you become a human being. These lives might include having lived as ants or other small creatures.

THINK ABOUT:

What do Sikhs believe to be the most important part of a person?

Do you have any ideas about what happens to you after death?

Why are Sikhs so grateful for their lives? How might they show this thanks?

When someone dies, the family may organise a complete reading of the Guru Granth Sahib.

Our holy book teaches that you should be so grateful for having a human life because this is the only life when you can do good deeds. You have the chance to live life to the full and sing God's praises.

We don't believe in burials, except for very young babies. Sikhs are always cremated. The important part of you is gone when you die. Your soul is gone, your spirit is gone, there is nothing important left. Your soul may be reborn in another body or it may be at peace with God, never to live in a body again.

If possible, the ashes will be taken back to India, but if not they should be sprinkled on running water. The family go to the cleanest part of a river, and a prayer is said. Only the family and maybe the priest will go to this ceremony. On the anniversary of a death, the family may hold a langar in memory of the person who has died.

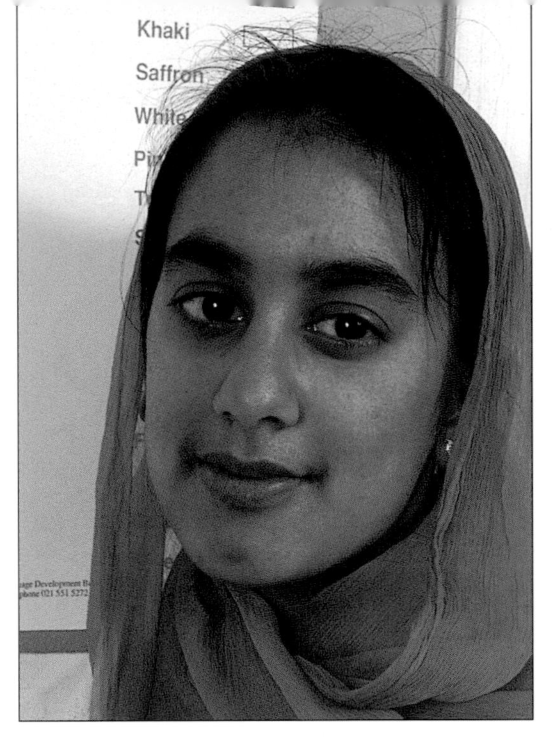

Neena: *A very good friend of the family, someone I'd known for all my life, died recently. When I heard that she had died I was disappointed and angry.*

Things to do

If you had the chance to live a life as another creature, what would you choose to be and why? Draw the creature and underneath write some reasons for your choice.

Try to explain in your own words what Sikhs believe about death and about what happens to a person's soul after death.

Neena felt angry and disappointed at the death of a friend. Draw a circle and in it write all the words you can think of which describe how someone might feel after the death of a close friend or relative. The words need not all be about sadness because you might believe in a better life to come. You could shade in the circle lightly using a colour of your choice.

Index

Page numbers in **black** *show*
Fact file *entries.*